Who Gets Amy's Room?

Jacqueline Rowe Coryell

Illustrated by Valerie Cordaro

Herrington House Press
3201 Lucerne St. NE
Albuquerque, NM 87111

Ordering Information: Discounts are available on quantity purchases by corporations, associations, and others. For details, contact the publisher at the address above.

Albuquerque, NM / Jacqueline Rowe Coryell, Author — First Edition

ISBN 978-0-9861604-4-8

Printed in the United States of America

Dedication

To Jerry, a real dad

Acknowledgements

Kim Jew, for making Amy feel beautiful;
the best photographer *ever* for caring so much

Kit, who takes care of people... family, friends, and strangers

Will, a caring and loving husband, father, and son

Liz, who only knows Amy as her guardian Angel

Dr. Ellen Kaufman, Kit's favorite doctor

Fletcher Miller School staff in Lakewood, Colorado who, for six years,
loved Amy and helped her grow beyond her handicaps

The Manzano School Side-by-Side staff in Albuquerque, New Mexico,
who welcomed Amy with open arms

Peggy Herrington, who took on Amy and me, to share our family story,
with a tear in her eye and warmth in her heart

Contents

Who Gets Amy's Room? 1

About Amy 41

Amy Gwendolyn Hudgins 43

Amy's Mother 44

About the Illustrator 47

About the Author 49

"Parenting the Handicapped Child"
Talk by Jacqueline Rowe Coryell 51

Who Gets Amy's Room?

My sister died.
It was a big surprise.
It was not a nice surprise.
It made me feel all tight inside.
So tight my tummy hurt.

Mom went into Amy's room and

got Amy's favorite pink dress.

And the dress-up shoes Amy wore with only

that dress

I asked, "What are you going to do with Amy's crayons?"

"You can have them if you want," mom said.

"What about Amy's Michael Jackson record?"

"I think I'll put that away for now," she said.

"Who gets Amy's room?" I asked.

My big sister's name was Amy.

She was 17 and rode the bus to the big high school.

She was handicapped.

Sometimes it was hard for our family.

Sometimes we fought.

Sometimes we were the best of friends.

Just like brothers and sisters everywhere.

Amy woke up sick yesterday.

Her temperature was 102.

Mom gave her aspirin and orange juice and sent her to bed.

My brother, Will, and my baby sister, Liz, played with me, Kit.

We laughed and swam, and had friends over.

We stayed home because Amy didn't feel good.

After swimming, my mom asked if we could go to their house.

Mom wanted to take Amy to see the doctor before the office closed.

After a while, my dad came and took us home.

We went swimming.

I like swimming with dad, he's so much fun.

We waited for Amy and mom to come home and fix dinner. Instead, mom called.

Dad had us get dressed again and took us back to our friend's house.

I was a little bit worried. Dad was, too.

It got late and my friend's mom had us go to bed.

Then mom and dad came back.

It was hard to go to bed when we got home.

Will and Liz were still asleep. But I couldn't.

Mom and dad couldn't either.

My dad and I talked.

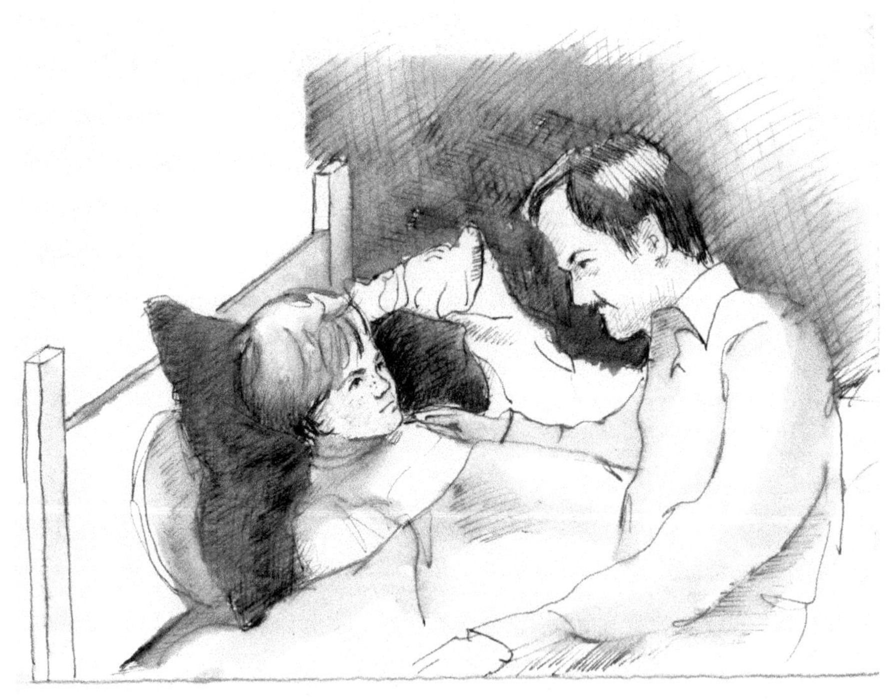

I asked my dad, "Where's Amy?"

He said, "She died, Kit.

"She was real sick and her heart stopped."

I cried.

"But I loved her a lot!"

My dad said, "I know, we all loved Amy."

Dad is good to talk to.

He understands what 8-year-old boys feel.

Sometimes it is hard to talk to mom.

But dad understands.

Mom and dad made lots of telephone calls.

I sat on the couch under one of grandma's afghans to keep warm.

I was cold.

Mom and dad told everyone about Amy.

And why she died.

And they cried a lot.

Then we all went to bed.

I was afraid.

So, I made a nest on the floor next to dad.

My mom got up real early.

And made more telephone calls.

In the dark.

I had hoped it was a bad dream.

But it wasn't.

Will is just 5 and when he got up,
my dad told him about Amy.

Will cried, too.

Dad said grandma and grandpa were coming to be with us, and he and mom had to go to the funeral home to make arrangements for Amy.

We were going back to my friend's house.

I wanted to go with dad.

I was afraid. I don't know why.

But that bad feeling was in my tummy.

Dad said I couldn't and they would be back real soon.

And they were.

The telephone was always busy.

Lots of people came over with food.

And flowers. And hugs.

And my grandma and grandpa came.

I'm grandma's boy.

I want to be close to someone—
with my dad and grandma, mostly.

Will wants to go play with Brandon.

He's too little to understand.

Grandma says she wants to get flowers for Amy.

I do, too.

Will says he does, too.

So, we go with grandma to the flower shop.

I have enough money for 2 pretty flowers.

The lady says they are carnations.

Will has enough money for 1 carnation.

The lady wants to put our flowers together.

I tell her I want my flowers by themselves.

Mom says Amy's father is coming.

I have never seen him.

I thought my dad was really her father.

He loves her and takes care of her.

That's what makes a real dad.

We get all dressed up.

I wear my blue suit.

And we go to the funeral home.

I'm frightened.

Mom looks nervous.

And we go to see Amy.

How can you see someone who is dead?

Will and I come in with grandma.

I'm a little scared and a little curious.

Grandma cries. Will and I look at Amy.

She has her pink dress on.
I can't see her shoes.

Grandma says to put our flowers in the casket with her.

We are a little afraid.

But grandma says it
is
all right.

So we put our flowers
in with Amy.

Amy looks different.

Mom says that is because our Amy is with God.

And that is just her body left behind.

Something about a soul.

I don't understand...

I just want to be with grandma.

Will and Liz go to another friend's house for dinner.

A lot of grownups come.

They say nice things.

And one man said, "She's at rest."

When my mom said, "She had better not be,"

he looked at her funny.

Mom said, "Amy is whole and happy and not handicapped anymore.

"She's doing all the things she could never do before.

"And she's with our grandma who died."

That makes mom feel a lot better.

Uncle Steve came.

Amy loves Uncle Steve special.

Just like I love grandma special.

And Will loves grandpa special.

Today is the funeral. I'm nervous.
My tummy gets tight thinking about it.

Everyone gets all dressed up but Will.

He doesn't want to go. So, mom calls Brandon's mom and Will goes to their house.

I have my blue suit on again.

There are lots of people at the chapel.

I think I'll walk around outside with Margie and Liz.

When I go into the chapel I sit with grandma.

Grandma cries a lot. Me, too. I miss Amy.

We go with the casket and everyone out to the grave.

It looks nice.

But I'm sad and I'm crying.

I tell grandma I want to go home.

And she takes me.

Lots of people come to our house
after the funeral.

They talk and eat.

Things don't seem so sad now.

Then they go home.

And Will comes home.

And it is only grandma and grandpa
and Uncle Steve.

And Uncle Virgil and Aunt Gin who flew in special
today.

They all talk and answer the telephone and eat.

Then everyone goes home.

And it is only us.

Will cries because he doesn't want to go to bed.

Mom tells him that no one else is going to die.

She says, "I promise."

Will feels better.

And goes to sleep.

But I am still worried.

When we see Dr. Kaufman for my checkup, mom tells her about Amy.

Dr. Kaufman says she is so sorry. "What happened?"

Mom tells it all over again.

Dr. Kaufman nods and says, "Kit, I am really sorry about your sister.

"Are you worried that might happen to you?"

I cry and nod my head.

Dr. Kaufman says, "Kit, Amy had a special problem. You don't have this special problem so this can never happen to you."

I feel a lot better. I think I was afraid I'd die too. But I couldn't say it.

Mom took Amy's things out of her room.

She put some in a box in the garage.

She gave some to the Children's Clothing Bank.

She gave some to the All Faith Children's Receiving Center.

And she made Amy's room into a playroom for us.

So Amy's room is a happy, fun place.

We all got Amy's room.

Amy is my sister.

Amy died.

I love her.

She is in heaven with God and grandma.

She's happy and healthy and having fun.

And watching over us.

About Amy

Amy Gwendolyn Hudgins
January 2, 1967-August 6, 1984

Born at Fort Knox, Kentucky, Amy was a lovely child, friendly and bright. On June 2, 1972, mom and Amy were getting ready to move to Florida, where mom had transferred with the telephone company. When Amy saw a friend she wanted to say good-bye to, she ran into the street, in front of a car and was run over. Leading to partial paralysis on the right side including right cheek, arm, and leg; brain damage causing epilepsy, behavior problems, and retardation; loss of her spleen and part of her liver and pancreas. Eight weeks in a coma, then therapy. After a year, mom was talking with a therapist and said she had wanted to move prior to the accident, and now couldn't, he said, "Don't you think they have doctors anywhere else?"

We moved to Denver, Colorado. In the Denver school system, they would call when her Special Ed class had a substitute teacher, telling mom to keep her home. Mom was unable to find reliable child care and had to quit her job, enrolling in college and taking classes when Amy was in school.

After Jacie met and married Jerry, the new family moved to Lakewood, which had schools for handicapped kids. We were invited to bring Amy to the Fletcher Miller School and leave her for a day. When mom went to pick her up, the principal said Amy had had problems during the lunch period, throwing her tray and acting out, mom was prepared that they'd sent Amy away. But the principal said, "We think Amy belongs here."

It was a wonderful school, fully staffed with teachers and therapists. As all the kids were different, no one was special, so everyone was treated the same.

We moved to a house with a pool in Albuquerque. Our Amy now had siblings, two brothers and a sister. Amy had matured and was a happy teenager. She loved having a baby sister and brothers and Daisy Dog. She went to the Manzano High School Side-by-Side program.

Occasionally, her brother Kit was put in charge of her, such as walking her to the bus stop, which annoyed her to no end. Amy did everything the rest of the kids did: chores, watching over the toddler, playing. That year, she had a date for the prom.

Amy is buried at Gate of Heaven cemetery.

Amy's Mother

By Jaqueline Rowe Coryell

When writing about Amy as a person, I found I was blocked. While looking for her death certificate, I came across the sympathy cards and letters we had received, and felt the statements from people who spent a lot of time with Amy told more about her. I had not read these missives since they had arrived many years ago. Jerry and I are still deeply touched by what these people said. These were the people who took her from being a frustrated child to a loving teen.

Comments from Sympathy Cards

"I enjoyed having Amy in the library throughout her years at Miller. She was always enthusiastic and fun to be with. All of us here have fond memories of her," wrote the Miller School librarian.

"She touched our hearts very much," wrote a neighbor.

"Amy will always remain in our hearts and minds... for her sweet personality and sensitivity to the needs of others," wrote a Miller Teacher.

"It meant so much to her to move with her family. She had a lot of happy times and a lot of love in her heart," wrote the Miller Principal.

"Amy used to have lots of friends plus I liked her from the beginning. At the end, my feelings turned sad inside 'cause I wish she was still living," wrote a Miller Classmate.

"I watched Amy grow from a little girl to a lovely young lady. It was exciting to see so many positive changes taking place," wrote a Miller Teacher.

"I know Amy was happy just being with her family," wrote a Miller School Bus Driver.

"Almost every day last year, she and her good friend Catherine would come into the office. Suddenly, I would look up and here would be these two blond angels, holding hands. Smiling, asking me if someone had turned in a piece of jewelry one of them had lost. We never found what they were looking for but I always looked forward to seeing those good kids coming by to say hello," wrote Manzano School Special Ed Secretary.

"I will always remember her happy and enthusiastic," wrote a Church Volunteer Teacher.

"Amy was a joy to have in class," wrote a Church Volunteer Teacher.

"I have prayed for Amy every night since the accident—12 years, such a long time," wrote Great Aunt Nesta.

About the Illustrator
Valerie Cordaro

A long-time resident of New Mexico, Valerie Cordaro has been a painter for over 40 years using a variety of mediums and subjects.

Painting and drawing people and children was her first focus. She did many small sketches of children for friends in addition to larger portraits.

Working with watercolor, pen, pencil, oil pastel and paints, she has done interiors, still lifes and landscapes. She donated 16 large portraits of women to Lovelace Women's Hospital in Albuquerque where they are on display throughout the lobby.

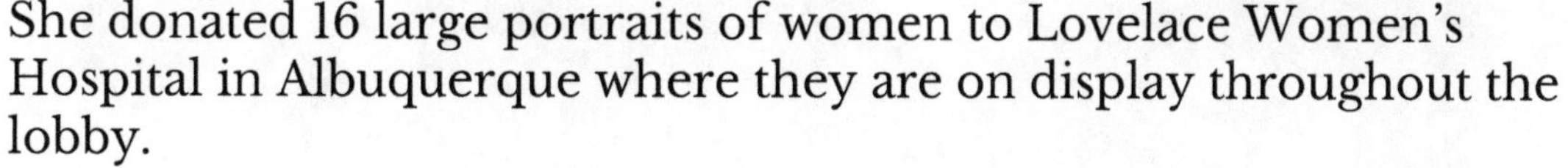

Currently, Valerie and her husband live in Albuquerque's south valley where they have extensive flowers, gardens and trees. They also have five delightful grandchildren to keep them busy.

She had never illustrated a book before, but says spending time with Jacie and her family was a pleasure. Valerie captured the distinctive essence of the story.

Learn more about Valerie and her art at www.valeriecordaro.com.

About the Author
Jacqueline Rowe Coryell

Photo by Steven Frankel

Born in Louisville, Kentucky, Jacqueline Rowe Coryell (AKA Jacie) lived in several states since her father was in the Air Force. Her mother and two brothers were killed by a drunk driver in Dallas, 1960. Jacie joined the Army WAC after high school, and later used her GI Bill benefits to graduate from Metropolitan State College in Denver, Colorado. In 1977, she became a leader at La Leche League, whose mission is to help mothers worldwide breastfeed through mother-to-mother support, encouragement, information, and education, and to promote a better understanding of breastfeeding as an essential element in the healthy development of the baby and mother. She especially enjoyed working with new moms and babies.

While in LLL Jacie became a conference coordinator, and later, as a member of the New Mexico Breastfeeding Task Force, managed their conferences for 10 years, retiring in 2013. She was a board-certified lactation consultant for 20 years, and for 25 years had a home business, Breastfeeding Resources. She enjoyed a two-year stint as a travel agent, specializing in Costa Rica and Paris, about which she says, "the travel perks were awesome."

Jacie believes implicitly in JFK's "ask not what your country can do for you, but what you can do for your country." She has spent her adult life as a community volunteer: La Leche League for over 35 years, and the NMBTF for 28. Jacie was a Girl Scout leader, Boy Scout popcorn mom, soccer referee, Little League score keeper, and she volunteered for 25+ years at Musical Theatre Southwest in Albuquerque.

A member of DAR, Jacie stays busy with genealogy, sewing (she made Liz's wedding gown), scrapbooking (way too many pictures!), and much more. Having traveled extensively, her dream is to spend a month in Venice and take an around-the-world freighter cruise. She is currently finishing as many projects as possible, including managing her own estate sale on eBay. ("Your kids should NOT have to clear out your lifetime of keepsakes.")

Jacie is married to Jerry, a kind and loving husband, who can fix just about anything. He even bought her a new car that matched her nail polish! How good is that?

All their children are now grown and have their own little ones. Jerry is still a real dad, and now, a real gramps.

Having written many short motivational articles, Jacie has carried only one book in her heart—and this is it.

Talk by Jacie Coryell
La Leche League International Conference1985
"Parenting the Handicapped Child"

I am the parent of a handicapped child, said Jacie Coryell in 1985. Amy was born a normal, healthy child. But when she was five years old, Amy dashed in front of a parked car into traffic, and was hit. The only reason she lived is that a police car was the next vehicle in line. We were at the hospital within 10 minutes of the accident.

Amy was in a coma for two months, during which time I was told she would be a vegetable. When she started coming out of the coma, we were all thrilled and joyfully accepted the return of our Amy. As a young, divorced mother I thought everything after that would be the same—we would simply be recovering.

Unfortunately, my Amy did not return. A different child, one who was retarded, who had social and emotional problems, was paralyzed on one side and, due to the loss of organs, a child who faced many challenges in the coming years.

I speak for parents who, like me, have enjoyed a normal baby or child that suddenly became handicapped. I think the sense of loss is just as strong, but losing a healthy child is dramatically different than having a baby born with a handicap. We had a normal child for several years when Amy's tragedy struck. I felt like the old wives' tale, The Troll Child: Trolls took my child and left a different one in her place (see page 55), and nothing I could do would get her back. I was expected to lavish the same love and attention on a different child.

Eventually, a variety of professionals told me in no uncertain terms that this was it for Amy. I could hope for no more. At that point,

I gave up. From then on, I experienced emotional problems from having a handicapped child suddenly thrust upon me.

While I had a strong marriage by then, and a supportive husband, I spent many years in turmoil. I sought professional advice at various times, and most of it was helpful. And I did place Amy in foster care for four years.

Through those years, with counseling and sharing experiences with other parents of handicapped children, I have reached several conclusions I would like to share with others who find themselves in similar situations:

1. It is not your fault. Whatever happened—if you were driving the car, left the stove on—whatever, it is not your fault. Things happened. A book that can help you is *When Bad Things Happen to Good People.*
2. Accept and love your child. That love and acceptance will affect the quality of life for you, the child and your family.
3. Don't accept the handicap, diagnosis, or limits. Always push for more; there may not be a cure but "Reaching for the Stars" should be your goal. Encourage your child, search for groups, organizations, teachers, whomever, to help you reach that goal. Many families have started businesses to develop a future job for their child. My Amy wanted to work for a hamburger chain. But some don't hire the handicapped in general, because they want all their employees to be able to do all the different jobs. I kept wondering why she couldn't have mopped floors and cleared tables. I think we could have found a special manager who would have worked with her. (Things have changed a lot since I wrote this in 1984.)
4. Don't accept an end to progress, don't let a social worker or counselor tell you your child will not be able to learn beyond a certain level. They can and will—they'll surprise you. Don't give up. Giving up will eat at you every day and you will have many regrets.
5. Share your life with others. If you become entirely wrapped up in your child, you will neglect yourself, your other children, your spouse, marriage and more. Instead, let them help you. Take time for yourself. I knew many families who found the stress was just too much. Extended families are important.

6. If you planned more children, have another baby. When I had anamniocentesis for my last baby, I heard criticism from everyone with normal, healthy children, but only support and understanding from those with handicapped children. A new baby takes the pressure off the handicapped child. Amy loved the babies and was very protective of them. She had time to sit for hours teaching a toddler how to stack blocks or color, and later she spent hours listening to them read.
7. Keep things as normal around your house as possible. Engage with friends who both do and don't have handicapped children. Most of my friends did not, but we helped them be more accepting of handicapped children.
8. There are people who will love your child with no restrictions. Cherish them.
9. And there are people who will say stupid things, such as "whenever I get discouraged about my family or like, I just think about you, and that makes me feel better about my situation." Either ignore it, develop snappy comebacks, or drop them. I live by this quote but don't recall where I read it: "It took many years for me to realize I had a choice about who I let touch my life and that I could surround myself with those who had a positive influence and let go of those who didn't."
10. Take your child to the best photographer in town for photos. A caring photographer will help you glimpse the special child within. Amy died about three months after her last photographs (some are in this book). I cherish them.
11. Hate the handicap but not the child. The best advice I received from another mother was, "It's okay to be angry. Go to your room and throw pillows, cry and rage in the shower, just don't take it out on your child." Did you know that many handicapped children are abused? Be sure to seek help the first time you lose control.

Amy died suddenly. One day she was fine, and the next day she wasn't feeling well. That evening she died. It was a shock to us all. It was also a relief: it was over.

But, you know, I think of Amy just as frequently now and in a positive light. Amy is still part of our family—we count her birthdays. I don't feel bad talking about her, but others are sometimes embarrassed. People don't feel comfortable talking about the dead.

My regrets: I wish I could have looked on her as a companion, and I always wonder if I could have done more. But even with the tough times we had I still love her, and my idea of heaven is that she knows of my love.

PETER AND THE TROLL BABY

Excerpt

In the deep of night in the dark room he shared with Susanna, Peter heard something.

He thought he saw bright red eyes blinking at him.

He hid under his blanket, slowly counting to ninety-nine.

Falun (the dog) whimpered.

Shuffle... shuffle...

Soon all grew silent.

At daybreak the baby bawled, screeched, kicked.

Peter got up to comfort her.

"THAT'S NOT MY SISTER!" he gasped—and ran to fetch his parents.

Side by side they stood and gazed at the red-faced thing.

Father said, "She's probably teething."

Mother said, "Of course it's Susanna. She has a tummy ache."

She picked her up. "She is heavy."

"This is my fault," mumbled Peter.

"I never should have wished it. Trolls can't help stealing, can they?"

"They are famous for it," said Father.

Note: This delightfully illustrated book by Jan Wahl is sadly out of print—though you might find a used copy online. Published in 1984 by Goldencraft, it's written in the manner of Grimm's fairy tales; the narrator, a young boy, becomes a hero, but retains a shred of doubt about his frustrating baby sister.